Atlas of our Birth

Serina Allison Hearn

Atlas of our Birth
©2010 by Serina Allison Hearn

ISBN 978-0-9817334-7-0

WOODLEY PRESS

Woodley Memorial Press
Washburn University
Topeka, Kansas 66621
Printed in the United States of America .

Edited by Dennis Etzel Jr.

First Edition

© Cover painting and concept: Timmia Hearn Feldman
Cover design-format: Justin Shiney

Atlas of our Birth

Do we not then have a responsibility, each and every one of us, to decolonise ourselves from imposed history, and situate ourselves within the history of humanity, each with our own personal histories in time and space participating in the infinite re-creation of the universe?

Vera Mihailovich-Dickman
Introduction to "Return" in Post-Colonial Writing
A Cultural Labyrinth

To Timmia, Zoey, Kaia, Jude,
and all children,
who carry the seeds of multiculturalism
necessary to reinvent the world.

Forward

I am honored to be the editor of this amazing work about place, the environment, colonialism and its current path, and family. *Atlas of Our Birth* is a map of an ongoing journey beginning in Trinidad and Tobago and includes Kansas. We are lucky to be a part of this poetic trip.

Being a native Kansan, I did not know much about Trinidad and Tobago before I met Serina Allison Hearn. Maybe they are part of the Caribbean Islands? As an American, I think about the genocidal and anti-environmental effects colonialism had on North and South America, but I never think about elsewhere — how Columbus also "discovered" and named Trinidad in 1498, how the Arawak and Carib Indians were mostly wiped out, then assimilated. The British took the island region from the Spanish in 1797, while prior to that there was much French influence. Trinidad and Tobago did not become independent until 1962. Its present constitution was only ratified in 1976, the bicentennial year of The United States of America's independence.

But these are the facts. I learned about T&T through Hearn herself, through her storytelling, her poetry—her voice. Her poems about the islands are more than a post-colonial recollection; they are a deep resonance of the past: "My father was already extinct when he was born, / but no one told him of this birth defect." The reader becomes the witness of how a white British system of sugar barons fell, and how it feels to leave such a place known as home:

> Yes, the body can walk away from its origins,
> can wave good-bye, put the heart under house arrest,
> lose its way on duty's road, pretend
> it knows where it is going, assimilate,
> become Buddhist, can board a Boeing 747

Leaving this place, the old Trinidad is a kind of warning for how our collective use—need—of limited resources as consumers is leading us to consuming ourselves.

However, these fierce poems are beautiful. They also feature Hearn's current home, Kansas and the prairie—another limited resource. They are poems of discovery, of a divorce, and of connection. Sometimes, we are pulled back to history, how there is still slavery and injustice on the path the Western world created, with "a million immigrant workers," and women "lured and trapped" into the sex slave trade as the USA and 121 nations are included.

Atlas transforms from memoir into a work of political activism and awareness.

On another note, one thing that pulled my heart into this work was how the role of "mother" figures in not just Hearn's life, but in our lives, too. As readers, we have the honor in sharing Hearn's experiences of motherhood:

> I want to give my daughter
>
> a magical amulet;
> the kind one finds in the best fairy tale
>
> when the heroine is rewarded
> for bravery.

We long for the best for our children, while being aware of the lack of our capabilities. Hearn is sincere and honest without being sentimental. Soon she'll be on that plane, that train, that boat,

> [S]he'll walk through those sliding doors
>
> into that waiting room for young travelers;
> like the first explorers who sailed into the unknown
>
> hoping to discover new worlds, she'll wave good-bye

These bold poems of memoir are a glimpse of fascination, of the courage to make a choice: "today and today and today we can choose to choose." They reflect my fascination with Hearn, as she is candid, open, and a force of change—a town crier turned to the world, to us.

With deepest thanks
Dennis Etzel Jr.

April 2010

Acknowledgements

Coal City Review: *Musing Again, No Sound was Heard,*

Artificial Selection, Goddess, Holding your Breath

Imagination Place Press: *Transplant*

Helicon 9 "Red and Black" : *Rich*

Seveneightfive: *The Story of Islands, Caught*

Ad Astra: *Restored Victorian, Displacement*

Kansas City Star: *Child's Play*

219 Press: *Candlestick Maker and Me*

With special gratitude: to Timmia Hearn Feldman for her oil painting,
conceived for the cover, which eventually grew into a postage stamp
and for the many hours of discussion involved in creating the art work:
Justine Shiney for his hard work and patience in making the cover a
reality: Zoey Hearn Feldman for her expert advice on photoshop and
for being a source of inspiration when she began her journey with maps:
Brian Daldorph for his years of poetry support, copy editing, and friendship.

Alicia Chance and James Conner, of Lawrence, Kansas, who allowed
the use of their impressive collection of British Trinidad and Tobago stamps
to illustrate this book.

Tony Backus who kept the wood-stove stoked all winter, the dishes
clean, and whose cooking gets better and better.

To withdraw Contents, cut Envelope across this line.

NOTICE.

The Registration Fee for a Letter, either inland or Foreign, is 2d. The sum paid for that stamp is that of the Registration Fee.

No Letter, addressed to a place outside Trinidad, can be accepted for Registration

If it contains Coin, Jewel, or precious articles.

If any investigation is required to be made about this Letter, the Envelope must accompany the complaint.

I never feel I have arrived, though I come
To journey's end. I took the road
That loses crest to questions, yet bears me
Down the other homeward earth

A Shuttle in the Crypt
Wole Soyinka

Looking at Her

One

Atlas of My Birth

Two

Where To Call Home

Three

FIRST FLIGHT

TRINIDAD—BATHURST—
LAGOS—LEOPOLDVILLE

TRINIDAD TO LAGOS

Angel

Four

They Call It Freedom

Five

One

Looking at Her

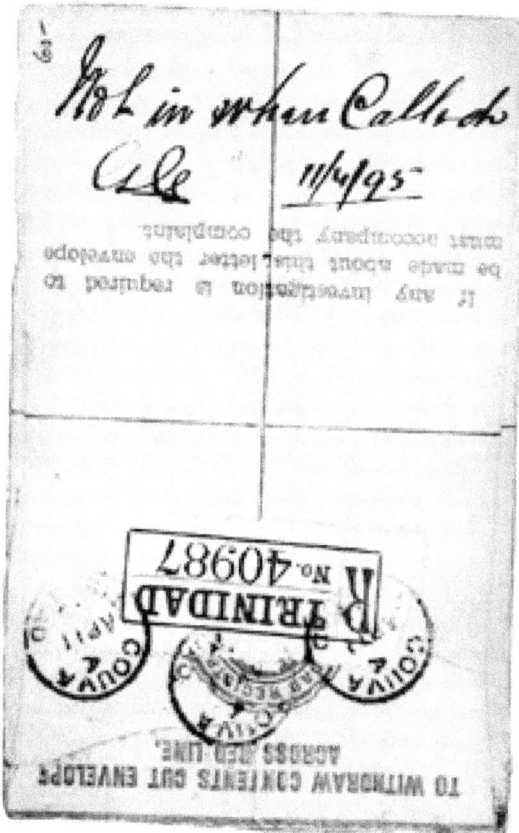

Not in when called on: Note from postman, on registered letter 1892.

Tobago, 1889, stamp of **Queen Victoria,** produced by De La Rue in Britain.

Tobago was occupied by indigenous people when Columbus sighted it on his third voyage in 1498. It was ignored by the Spanish until 1629 when Dutch merchants established a colony and brought enslaved Africans to work the land. Located 20 miles (32 km) off the northeast coast of Trinidad, this tiny island, 116 sq. miles in area, was regarded as a prize. For the next 200 years, Tobago **changed hands 33 times** between the Spanish, the Dutch, the English and the French, all of them rival colonists. In 1763, Tobago was ceded to Britain, it was then captured by the French in 1781 and then recaptured by the **British in 1793**. The island was finally ceded to Britain in 1814 by the Treaty of Paris. On **April 6, 1889,** Tobago was annexed administratively to Trinidad - on the insistence of the British Government in an effort to secure more financial stability.

Looking At Her

Was Eve's day like mine?
A day like any other in paradise:
Sky translucent water colour,
the garden fragrant with cinnamon,
bay-leaves, nutmeg...

As she glanced around that fateful day,
sun jeweled the dewy lotus buds,
bird chorus thrilled the leaves
breezy kisses hummed
and she must have thought her world secure.

So was it false bravado on her part?
A fundamental inability to perceive such a thing
as consequences? She had been warned:
disobeying would lead to great suffering;
but what was suffering?

I can only think that the serpent must have
taken her off guard with his charm,
his witty sense of humor, his teasing logic:
Why not explore? Why not self-determine?
From trial and error comes knowledge,
and curiosity is the only antidote to boredom.

I feel her heart beat louder, her mouth water,
and sudden heat surge toward her fingertips;
as if she had no will, had made no choice,
but did the only thing she could:
bring the fruit to her mouth and bite down hard...
Somewhere in the distance I can hear God laughing.

Musing Again

The Muse says what I think matters,
if I listen quietly
voices will come;
tell what's inside my heart,
but the last time I listened to my heart
I almost lost my head.

I tell the Muse:
It doesn't take much to hack through
bone and sinew or mother from child,
one second my blood surged like high tide,
next, I would lose even the feeling of myself
as finite as a grain of sand.

The Muse says that I have only one life,
think about myself before anyone else.
Can my family be happy
when I am not fully fledged?
But even those on wing cannot stay forever high
and dusk brings with it shadows cast by other suns.

The Muse strokes his flame-singed hair
and says, I shall keep you young if you will follow
through forest green, up hill and dale;
leave your duties, your worries,
and free your mind
so that I may fill you up and make you mine.

Faux Finish

With sea sponge
and lambs wool
I caress you,
massage grape red,
wine red,
poinsettia fusion
with mulberry red,
lips deep as garnets,
I paint supernova;
pleasure surprises
the straight face
of your living-room wall.

Long Distance

Ah, well, that is how it is, and that is the mystery.
Spencer Brown on his book *Laws of Form*

I take the white bouquet of moon-flowers
you had delivered
and put them in the blood red vase
you gave me last year:
Remember you found it on the reject shelf
in Murano where men breathe life
into molten glass?
I laughed and said it was a biography
of my own misshapen heart.
We reminisce about hours spent
in bed reading:
Your voice taking me by the hand
down the Orinoco
to listen to Lokono stones sing;
then you tell me that making love
is god's way of communicating with us
"For where two... are gathered
                in my name there am I..."
Inside the universe of principia-principii
you see me
standing against a dark doorway
one foot up on the threshold
the other on the cobble-stone pavement,
the wind is blowing scraps
down the alley,
and you put your hands
up my skirt, my imaginary skirt,
and we pray.

No Sound was Heard

Love came
down
wet,
wet,
wet,
Palm fronds,
Mango,
Sapodilla,
trembled,
dripped over ferns,
Dido orchids, Bird of Paradise…
stems, limbs, large trunks,
swayed and bowed
heaving under sky's tumid weight,
music poured.
Parched Earth
drank,
drank,
drank,
until fruit,
ripe and full,
dropped softly
to their forest bed.

Undressing

Let me take my skin off for you,
let me peel off my hair,
let me pull out my cracked heart,
my gridlocked brain,
constricted lungs,
bitter liver,
my weakened kidneys...
I will even take off
my finger and toe nails,
discard it all,
so I can become clouds
that caress the valleys
of your emerald forest.
I will dissolve into rainwater
and run down gullies to your ocean;
I will be mangrove roots
dancing in a fusion
of earth, sea and heavens;
I will be the rolling tides
that come and go across the shoreline
of your island;
I will be wind that blows
the night stars across the orbit
of your moon.
I will coo with pigeons
outside your heart's window;
I will be the Poui blossoms
blanketing the ground
upon which you walk;
I will be the air you breathe,
the coconut
in your drinking water,
the eye in the hurricane
of your longing.

All Day Long

He says laugh, she cries.
He has a wife,
she is one of his secrets.
He writes about God,
she is hard on herself.
He says we make our world,
she is ready to let the worms make her.
He says we must pray...

She says his name is an anvil,
striking, striking, love's second hand;
slow heartbeats count eternity
when he's gone,
while somewhere
a woman in the mountains
waits for her lover's return,
a woman on the hotel balcony
waits for his knock,
a woman in labor cannot cry his name.

Every woman is a different chord
in the chorus of song
singing his name,
wanting him, wanting him,
wanting liquid fire.
Yes, let us pray, she says,
pray to burn away,
until we are nothing but wind,
nothing but ashes,
nothing but the firmament
that binds together...
without trace.

The Story of Islands

Camouflaged amidst
creamy coconut smiles,
brown coco-butter cleavages,
dark chocolate cheeks
underpinned with desire's bone,
where dreams nestle on the snail tongue
of liquid love
silently creeping
across the drawbridge
to imprisoned passion,
whose lips wait parted,
whose blood navigates the moon,
whose whispers are heard
through ghost laughter:
Lovers past,
Lovers future,
Lovers too old
to miss the boat…
but it's already the last night
and isn't the story of paradise always
about leaving?

POSTED ON THE HIGH SEAS
ABOARD THE
S.S. ALCOA CAVALIER

The Measure of His Feet

Since you can't come to me
I will come to you;
dressed in Bird of Paradise,
Heliconia, from cool mountains,
will drape ruby perpendicular tendrils
around bare shoulders.
A blouse of anthurium coral pink
will cup my breasts,
I will crown myself your Josephine
with flaming torch and perfumed tuberoses.
I will sit on your office desk
where tomorrow's strategies are planned,
and open wide
my bouquet of cool evening breezes
to caress your conquest-weary head,
dismantle your armor-plated suit
and remind you of a time
when the yard rooster played piano,
a boy could fly,
and a man knew the pleasure
of his naked feet
in so many other ways
than to lead.

Question

He opens me when he needs,
raises the lid and there I am,
woman in a box,
writing long love letters
to fill the dark hours without his face;
when I see him, hear his voice,
I begin to sing:
Sometimes a sad song, filled
with a lone child's tears in the school yard
waiting, waiting for someone to remember
to take her home,
or it's the rain song
hammering, hammering roofs
below which sleeping lovers sigh,
belly to belly songs, lips to ear,
breath to breath, arm hollow to round cheek,
bones turned to honey under flame;
sunshine songs filtered through banana leaves
defused brilliance richer than emeralds on 5th Avenue,
ecstatic songs of racing clouds
and feet that never touch the ground,
breast songs full of love's milk
hot and hard with no release
except for pain who latches on
and won't let go...

      today you didn't come,
              didn't come...
and a lonely song, a murmur song,
whispers itself to me:
Why does the woman sing so sweetly
to he who keeps her
secret in a box?

Postcard to Hades

Now I carry you wherever I go
Even as I want to end the longing;
Soft and wild I grow.

Unwillingly, I loved you though:
Limb to limb, tongue to grove, even sleeping.
Now I carry you wherever I go.

I gestated a long time ago,
Your bitter, sweet, pomegranate seedlings,
Soft and wild I grow.

I wanted you to change the rules in your chateau,
But good-byes watered our newly bedded fruiting.
Now I carry you wherever I go.

You refused to come with me, grief's gone solo.
Remember our first wine, your smell intoxicating?
Soft and wild I grow.

You are my phantom, dark flambeau
Setting fire to reason's saplings.
Now I carry you wherever I go,
Soft and wild I grow.

22

Tidal

Fish of our Atlantic
will remember how
wave after wave we danced
waltzing the high tide,
our bodies enveloped
between undulating
rise and fall,
merged and emerging.

Fish of our bed
will remember
warm currents spiral
between river mouth and sea
in a melody of salt water,
fresh water,
merged and emerging,
we loved.

Fish of our dreams
will remember
how we forged up river
through dark swamp,
past heron, cayman,
mangrove and crab traps
merged and emerging,
we loved,
rose and fell.

Caught

Distance long-strokes the currents of my veins,
eyes, yours, softly butterfly my belly.

Once full-parted lips, patient, practiced,
surveyed the valley of my heart.

Caught in memory's hypnotic full moon,
I wait, like women trapped in earlier centuries

waited on men, they waited dressed in mourning,
a day, or a year, for the sea to bear them back:

The fine sediment of absence settling
along the banks of desire's tumultuous flow.

Large cities have been known
to be built on such accumulation.

Grim Fairy Tale

...he's more me than I am myself
Emily Bronte

Her tower was round and hard,
a spiral staircase wound its way
outside and entered the room
at the top,
where she sat all day
in her rocking chair
counting strands of years past;
the names of princes
who had come with gifts
but left her empty
so she spurned them all;
each one vowing never to return
while she sits and rocks
remembering her first love:
He had grabbed her hard,
gave her a mirror
in which she could look and see
all that she could be
with him,
and had told her
that no one could ever live up
to his great mind,
his passion,
or his undying love.
His promises
had already spanned a century
from the pages of a book,
written by a woman,
who'd never had a man,
about a man
who'd never existed.

Beloved

for Trenda Reschke

You have stood patiently
in rush hour's corridors
waiting for the beloved.
Wind howled centuries,
love letters chased around
canyon halls;
storms hammered the canopy above;
when the pragmatic sun came out
it bleached the inside
till your heart came to resemble
hollow vaulted caves
carved in petrified currents
of desert rock.
Suddenly
through an unexpected fissure,
one tender ray of light
fell into that polished,
empty,
waiting room.
Weathered and worn,
you saw the beloved's face;
it was your own.

SHIP-LETTER
TRINIDAD

Field of Atoms

Don't listen to this,
because if you do you will find
yourself hiding with me
behind words
which in the end
is only sound trying
to imitate breath
going in
and coming out,
my voice saying these words
is a ploy to cover up breath,
going in and coming out,
this pounding heart
is so that breath might go
in and come out,
and if I tell you I want
to wrap my imaginary arms
around your imaginary neck,
this too is only distraction from my breath
going in and coming out,
my imaginary legs entwined in yours
is nothing more than my breath going in
and coming out,
this here and now,
this distance between us,
is nothing more than an illusion
of time;

there is no time,
there is only breath
going in and coming out,
and if I say I miss you,
it is yet another phrase to hide behind,
a feeble attempt to distract from the utter
aloneness...
and if you have listened this far,
then remember,
it was only a diversion,
a hiding,
a momentary fluctuation in the field of atoms.
The fact is
we're not here,
just a dream in the landscape
of a great sleeping planet
that need not breathe at all
but spins endlessly
in the ever expanding universe
of silence visible.

PAN AMERICAN WORLD AIRWAYS
FIRST DIRECT CLIPPER FLIGHT
NEW YORK TO PORT OF SPAIN

Two

Atlas of our Birth

Columbus is described, in a Eurocentric view of history, as having discovered Trinidad on the 31st, July, 1498, during his third voyage. He was not, however, the first on the island, as many native peoples called it home. His "discovery" led to the eventual subjugation and near extermination of the native peoples who called the island Iere: Land of the Hummingbird. Columbus was part of the Age of Exploration, a time in which Europeans felt that the world was for their taking. He, and others, failed to recognize that pre-agricultural indigenous groups from the Orinoco Delta of South America had first claimed Trinidad some 7,000 years before. However, Columbus' "discovery" marks the start of the region's modern history, and the subsequent importation of people's from around the world. Today, with an approximate population of 1.3 million, 39% of Trinidad's population is of African descent, 41% is East Indian, and the remaining 20% is comprised of a mix of Spanish, French, Portuguese, Italian, British, Chinese, Jewish, Syrian and Lebanese descent.

Britannia sits on bales of sugar with a ship in the background. This image first appears on stamps in 1851.

In 1860 the territorial extent of the British Empire had some 9.5 million square miles; by 1905 the total had risen to 12.7 million. The British Empire now covered 25 percent of the world's land surface and controlled some 44 million people. In 1924 it was estimated that the British Empire covered an area one hundred and fifty times the size of Great Britain itself, it was the most extensive empire in world history.

Temperature Reading

One degree outside,
wind-chill factor:
minus seventeen degrees;
layer upon layer of wool
and still cold.
My Scottish grandfather
sailed south one day
the scent of his future
African wife
filling his nostrils
with heat.

Atlas of My Birth

When my sepia brown grandmother fretted
because our *white-father smell* reminded her
of slave days she never endured,
I felt pity for her;
when my blond grandmother declared
"East could never meet West"
before my parents' marriage,
my un-conceived self asked for her forgiveness;
when my own country could not recognize me
as part of its equal heritage
and no one else would claim me as their own,
I learned to claim myself:
I befriended my sixteen great, great grandparents.
In love or not,
those 1850's women birthed their eight babies
on the soil of Portugal, Italy,
the West Indies, Scotland, England and China:
they who could already smell
the Atlantic of my birth;
as some prepared to leave Europe,
or were sea sick half way across the Indian ocean,
two already crossed over in slave-chains,
others fleeing drought, persecution,
or with Bible in hand dreamed of freedom,
bounty, and paradise.
Washed up on unknown shores
like ghosts from distant starlight,
all they wanted in the end
was that their children should live,
and their children's children.

The Twenty-Fifth Hour

Chaos and structure raged
around the centrifuge of my parents' war:
Father blown by Drake's legacy,
mother straight-jacketed
in coloured middle-class;
I survived on grandmothers' tropicals:
Great Gran the Leewards
and Gran the Westerlies;
sustained by Cumulus and Cirrus,
a bromeliad,
clinging high in the branches
of a Saman tree,
I vacillated between
Jehovah's Paradise Lost to come
or Satan's Kingdoms now?
On foreign continents
the clock strikes two o'clock twice —
daylight saving time.
I seize the question,
rearrange it and slip past
lamb and lion
across the checkered board
of black and white,
into uncharted reds, yellows,
blues, chartreuse
of Terra Incognita.

Passport

I am told to sit on a high stool
and face the white, blank screen.
The camera points straight,
I stare into its mechanical eye,
down into the passage of my arrival here.
I am video tape rewinding...
back to 2004,
past 1993...
the last time I needed renewing
my second daughter was just born
and I had begun to forget
      the girl in 1981
standing in a small booth
at Tottenham Court Road station
thinking, with resolution,
that she was sending her face,
like Voyager,
into the darkness they call solar system
in the hope of being found,
in the hope that we are not alone,
she stood in the small photo booth
and shot herself
so I could gain entry.

Straits of Magellan

She wanted the bougainvillea chopped down for safety,
she said; that way people can see the house and not think there is
anything worth stealing; besides when the iron fence rusts you can't
paint it if it has thorns and flowers misbehaving all over the railings
and pavement making it hard for people to walk past without being
interfered with.

He called the place Fort Knox with its iron bars over every
window and its extra security behind every bolted door. Though he
slipped in and out whenever he pleased. To where? No one knows. Not
in forty-six years of marriage did he ever tell where he went, when he'd
be back, though he always came back with his dirty clothes for her to
wash and an empty wallet.

She filled the house with artificial flowers. They never made a
mess and were dependable for their blooms. Photographs of grown
children smiled from every wall, except where he slept; they had
emigrated to hang where she slept on a cot in a corner of the guest
room; the undisturbed chenille-draped queen bed waiting for the next
visiting daughter, or son, from overseas.

He worshiped his mother. She held her photographed head, over
the master bed, and was beautiful like a haughty 1940's movie star, or
royalty. He loved to relate how once when the neighbours complained
she told them, *"When my cocks are out you keep your hens locked up....* We
laughed too bad, until naked in the shower, she plastered us all with a
leather belt and buckle."

She once dreamed she was lost on the Atlantic until she found
the Straits in my father's piercing eyes: a blue icy undertow of a legacy
in obsolescence: No more white people passport, not even enough
deer and agouti to hunt like the old days: crab scarce, scarlet ibis pale,

23

poinsettia December-red, vanished under a modern night filled with street lights.

While my mother's kind are anxiously industrious, drive imported new cars, engineer roads, build safe places to hide, keep the bush at bay, fuel the Ice Cap as it hemorrhages into the Straits of Magellan; and Magellan himself? Dead in the Philippines, 1521, long before his voyage was completed, because he failed to take the natives seriously along the reefs of Mactan Island.

Never Never Land

I am buying my father, I said.
He looked puzzled.
You see, my father is six years old
and married to my mother:
She worked hard
to pay bills,
feed children,
be there in the night.

He likes to pull wings off flies
which makes my five-year-old
mother cry.
She doesn't know
that she can tell him to stop
or walk away.
She cries.
He plays.

So I am bribing my father
with this fat check
to leave,
then I am getting them divorced.
Don't get me wrong
I love my father,
he gave me many gifts:
I, too, know
how to pull wings off flies.

Ill-Bred White Men

Old is when love is not enough
to save two drowning –
by saving my mother
my father drowns –
but I grieve,
for with him will go
the great visages of men
who conquered the horizons:

Planted and harvested the sugarcane,
cotton, wheat or oil.
Those ill-bred white men
who subdued the natives,
bartered in slaves,
reaped wealth for nations
and created chaos
to ferment the world.

Old is when I can predict
night falling like the chair beneath
a hanged man's feet.
The New World your kind
savagely helped birth
has long become unrecognizable:
without white man's privilege
or the overseer's ominous rule

All you have left
is the colourblind sun
turning one empty day into another
and memories

of your lost kingdom of El Dorado
where you were never king,
nor I your princess.

The Sun Never Sets

My father was already extinct when he was born,
but no one told him of this birth defect.
He was welcomed on the island; a sapphire-eyed,
blond emissary of England's ruling class:

He commanded his ragged army before dawn rose:
Bent over and sweating, like recent slaves before,
East Indian men, and women, harvested burnt cane with cutlasses,
bundled and loaded carts pulled by sullen bison.

Later Boss-man drank with these laborers who gathered
to talk agouti, deer, and the sweet sound of hunting dogs baying
on the scent. They laughed at his stupid jokes, humoured him
with their used women. In the morning his pockets were empty.

The sugar barons gave him a big estate-house, a gardener for his acre,
a drive lined with palm trees; you would have thought had you seen
him on his horse, or later in his Land Rover, perusing the endless
fields of Tate and Lyle, that he was in his prime.

Instead, he was an echo of a time gone by, his portrait hung
alongside other defunct servicemen in history's dusty hallways
of disgraced antiquity; their names, faces, a hostile curiosity
to the new independent, oil-rich, heirs about to face their own demise.

BUY
BRITISH EMPIRE
GOODS

The Candlestick Maker and Me

I had to leave behind rain
on one side of the street
sun shining on the other,
coconut carts around the Savannah,
Pommerac trees painting the ground fuchsia,
mountains flowering Poui yellow
at the start of dry season;
and sugar cane blooming for miles;
the Caroni river running down to the sea
and the sea always calling, calling...
I had to leave behind my childhood
for the winds of fortune
were blowing.

I had to leave behind the corner store,
the butcher, the baker and green grocer,
Camden High Street studio, Albert Street flat,
and youth's friends, my first home,
black cabs, double decker buses, the Tube;
English skies of tepid greys,
mossy greens to chartreuse heaths,
wild Foxgloves over Devon cliffs
and Regent's roses climbing midsummer,
Puck out to play...
I had to leave behind my second home
for the winds of fortune
were sudden.

I had to leave behind our well-laid plans,
the king-sized bed in Port Jefferson,
Toronto, Ann Arbor, Princeton,
and our final destination;
the children's symmetrical world,

and our final destination;
the children's symmetrical world,
dinner at six for four went up in flames,
long arguments at night.

What would Achilles choose?
The small back garden, large Victorian,
professor's wife, stability, health insurance?
I had to leave behind marriage
for the winds of fortune
were treacherous.

BY AIR MAIL

AIR LETTER

IF ANYTHING IS EN-
CLOSED THIS LETTER
WILL BE SENT BY
ORDINARY MAIL.

Reply to Christopher Marlowe (1563 – 1593) and Sir Walter Raleigh (1552 – 1618)

for Tony, Oct 15th, 2005

Though rocks grow cold
and frost's first kiss
wrinkles the bloom of spring,
autumn air still stirs
the saffrons, browns and crimsons
in my blood;
a tiny boat of green and jade,
blown by stubborn hope,
tacks back and forth
across time's seas
of mysteries deep and blue.

Yesterday is forever gone,
and tomorrow's not yet here,
but now, in this sap,
this leaf stem to wind, bow to horizon,
I flutter, I rejoice, I say thanks for
thy bed of roses...,
thy coral clasps
and amber studs...
I have seen them rot,
I've seen youth fade,
but I shall not forget.

And even with this heart of gall
daffodils can make me smile,
touch become harmonious
and every night all the stars,

so old, so bright,
shine on posies sweet,
as well as wanton fields;
and because I've learned
to embrace it all,
I choose today
to live on edge
and be your love
until we fall and break.

Housekeeping

I learned to keep order when I was young:

Anger	at my father when he bullied my mother,
Fear	when he took off his belt and said, *Come here*,
Rage	at grandmother who picked on my brother most,
Sadness	because mother cried every day,
Humiliation	because I wet the bed most nights,
Loneliness	of a child without friends,
Anxiety	that God would not approve of me,
Embarrassment	as we were the poor relations,
Hopelessness	because I did not know how I would get away.
	All I hid inside an old wooden trunk with a heavy lock
	behind veiled curtains woven with vivacious smiles.

When I did get away, I took the trunk with me, abroad,
kept it where it was easy to reach, put my first

Broken-heart	there, with his letters and photograph;
Inferiority,	the kind country people have when they go
	to the big city young and alone, was silenced.
Pride	went too, it didn't pay the bills, neither did
Failure,	those twins had to go;
Naiveté	was folded and
	set aside.
Religion	went slowly, an ancient city eroded by wind...

Today, I opened the box to put away the

Doldrums:	was surprised to find my children's
Innocence	wrapped neatly in yellowing paper,
	their father stared out from between black
	and white, the verdict:

Guilty

Dreams   embalmed in residue of

Despair

Laughter   and faded pansies were pressed between
                   pages of an old journal,

Conviction   scantily slept in moth balls;

Will-power   hid in a corner muttering…

Tears   blinded me and I quickly shut the lid.

Necessity   and I will go last, along with the trunk
                   they must burn,
                   until then

Spirit   will be my companion.
                   She is the thread that binds them all,
                   does not let me forget how

Joy   is a fresh breeze that can fill emptiness,
                   as I keep making order in the almost clean house
                   for my children.

Home Coming

*"Copperfield," said Mr. Micawber, "accidents will
occur in the best-regulated families; and in families
not regulated by . . .the influence of Woman..."*
[1850 Dickens, *David Copperfield* xxviii.]

The pinprick of blue fire
glowed faintly in the old man's eyes.
I held on to the fragile lifeline
of those dying embers,
holding steady,
as I worked my way through
the derelict ruins of his urban cave.
I had found him
in his ancestral home.
The house permeated
with festering pee-soaked trousers
and clothes piled high on, and around,
his ravaged mattress
which hadn't seen the grace of a sheet in years.
Right angled, he lay,
on the double bed,
marginalised by the accumulation of neglect
his feet dangled over the edge,
hands interlocked neatly across his bony chest.
He looked ready for a funeral pyre
but when I touched his grimy naked feet
he opened the window a crack
and the smoldering blue of his irises focused:
"Allison," he said,
straining into a sitting position,
"when did you get here?"

I helped him to his feet
and put my arms around him
"Hello, Dad" I said.
"How are you?"
"I'm okay," he replied in a far away voice.
I held his small frame in my arms
and lightly rocked the stiff
unyielding mirage of a man,
"I love you…" I said,
"I know" he replied.

BY AIR MAIL
PAR AVION

Artificial Selection

Turtle soup is still legend here
in Tobago, among the grandfathers
and grandsons.
Long line fishing up North
kills the other refugees.
Soon, Leatherbacks will be as extinct
as dinosaurs with whom
they once roamed;
though not long ago
you couldn't see Turtle Beach
for turtles.
Today, if you are lucky,
you might see one
emerge from the ocean
and lay her pearl white eggs
in the sands where she was born.

With the last of the Leatherbacks
I will, near sighted,
look for faint moon glow on waves,
make my slow and ponderous way
down to the final ocean;
not as Noah's chosen few
but as the great Dodo Bird,
the White Tiger of Bali,
or Aborigines of Paradise Lost:
with the keen scent of my native air ,
sea-salt coolness will kiss feet,

embrace open arms;
submerge eyes, then head...
and the secret knowledge of my kind, too,
will dissolve into the blackened deep
of history's footnotes.

TOO LATE

TRINIDAD
C
NO 24
84

Manifesto

for Winston Riley

Home is scarlet ibis, hummingbirds, Pitch Lake,
the broad-backed Saman tree. Paradise under siege
from plastic, Styrofoam, beer cans, assaulted coastlines;
howler monkeys and ocelots wait for rescue parties to arrive.

Home is friendly villages, safe towns, wide open Savannah;
grandmothers, sons and daughters labour under neglect,
drug trafficking, kidnapping, murder, and politicians
in love with the rum-punch of self-importance.

Homemakers, utilitarians, carpenters, gardeners, artists,
musicians are my peers not those dazed by materialism,
seduced by TV commercial fantasy into a frenzy of greed
and systemic blindness who follow destiny's Neanderthal.

Home is where backyard chandelier bush medicine
and coral-peach Mora trees crown mountains overlooking
seas that patron the navigational tenure of the mighty
Leatherbacks, who harness sun and waves.

Home is rain-forests, where mangroves filter pollution,
jungle stitches earth in place, floods subside, orchids bloom
wild and sugarcane's ghost sweetens the air; not this ill
planned concrete diaspora funded on depleting oil revenue.

Home is diversity; we rose, flying fish from seven bloody seas,
to become imagination's dancers; cross-pollinated hybrids
perched on natural selection's high wire who must choose
today and today, and today to choose choice, save our children.

Post Immigrant Recipe

I melt brown sugar in olive oil
until the fragrance of burning cane fields fills me.
I could never eat our hand-fed chickens that Granny killed,
twisting their necks with a quick motion of mercy;
but de-feathered and sealed in plastic
I have no problem peeling the skin from the pink flesh
and with precision searing them
in carmelised sweetness; then adding pounded garlic,
grated coco, finely chopped onions,
sweet bay-leaves from the century-old garden
of the Gingerbread House in Trinidad –
that fears the developer's ball and chain –
stirred in with Kansas neighborhood marjoram and thyme
and Bill's frozen pesto, as good as the day
he picked it months before he died,
carrots sliced in round orange
the colour of a full Prairie moon on horizon,
green peppers diced, pulped farmers-market tomatoes,
raisons sprinkled like crows in soybean landscapes,
sirens from the Caribbean Sea sing about hungry,
homesick men from Portugal, Spain and Africa;
I stir a cacophony of senses and ancestral memory
to evoke the distance bring it near.

The Watcher

Childhood fingers remember lovingly
stroking the scarce watercolour paper,
like a connoisseur I inhaled its possibilities,
understood its uncompromising invitation
to draw from its nakedness
a heron's secret as it lifts into flight,
or paint the heady intoxication
of a hummingbird as it descends
the spiral petal tongue of nectar.

Thin black lines waiting on blank pages,
held together with cotton and bedded between
hard covers, remained barren;
a virgin held in a trance I read lives
spun from pain, conflict, darkness, light, joy;
was anointed with others' epiphanies:
words bloomed meadows in my head,
while my heart-seed stayed silent
and watchful.

I remember how my body, young and innocent
was bartered by my own hands,
and signed the contract stating
I had become a stranger's wife,
so that I could escape;
how my untouched body laid itself down,
opened its unmarked pages for another
to autograph before I had had a chance
to name my own story, paint my own portrait.

Now old and inscribed with history's
timetables from foreign shores,

I am carried, dark like waves at sunset,
sleek and wet; wave after wave
compels to the beginning end,
the river's mouth, where a young girl has waited,
year after year, for the courage to claim her pen,
her paintbrush, her voice
and keep a promise.

RETURN TO SENDER

Birthright

*for Jean Rhys who went back too late
and for Antoinette who tried*

You never asked to be born with skin
like white cockroach in the West Indies.
If you could you would have dyed
yourself in coloured water,
washed the bruises off your forehead,
and rebirthed coco-butter from the ocean
with the right to belong to your island.

No one would blame you
for what others did, and you didn't,
your face would not be a symbol for hatred;
your white mother would not have been left for mad,
to be raped day after day by emancipated slaves.
No white man could marry you
for money, crush your identity.

Had you been born a slave descendant
you would have learned from your mother's milk
the art of rebellion, your naive faith
in goodness would have been shattered:
no polite society, no inheritance, no stranger
would take you across that dark Sargasso Sea;
you would have refused to go.

Instead you rose one freezing Bronte night
found flame to warm your courage
and dressed in red, set fire
to your prison; threw yourself
from the roof; surrendered your amnesia
to wings of obeah and flew home
to the land of the flamboyant tree,
that was yours, as much as theirs.

Carry On

The body can walk away,
can fold its possessions into a small carry-on;
engage in last minute checking for:
passport, green-card, phone-charger,
medication, a book to read on the long flight north
away from this island embryo
gestating in Caribbean-Atlantic seas,
yoked with history's labour pains that echo still
through weather-eaten wooden Victorians,
termite infested ginger-bread,
rusted galvanized roofs, wrecking crews,
the crazy man shouting in the street,
and the aroma of you and me breathing together
like sugarcane fields burning under pounding rain...

The body can walk away
from great grandparents who witnessed:
the first Asian indentured labourers arrive in ships
after slavery ended,
the first telegraph messages,
the first plane crash in Queen's Park Savannah,
the first steel-pan musicians play Beethoven;
the late twentieth century conquest
of high-rise architectural exile in concrete,
steel, glass, and greed;
air-conditioning brackets the fecund earth
which can no longer whisper through slated jalousies
secrets from rainforest bromeliads, giant ferns,
orchids, manicou and iguana...

Yes, the body can walk away from its origins,
can wave goodbye, put the heart under house arrest,

lose its way on duty's road, pretend
it knows where it is going, assimilate,
become Buddhist, can board a Boeing 747,
can carry folded between the disguise
of practicality an undetected ticking bomb
close to detonation, can weep
with its head bowed to the plane's window,
blind to the parceled land below
for sale to the highest bidder,
blind to the indifferent nomadic clouds
that engulf;
can weep for the dead and dying
and those who will never know what was,
it can shake like the last leaf in fall....

BUY
TRINIDAD
SUGAR

Three

Where to Call Home

8th June, 1946, Houses of Parliament, London, England: Victory Celebrations of Commonwealth & Empire after the defeat of Nazi Germany and Empire of Japan in World War II under King George VI's reign.

This stamp was an omnibus issue, which is any group of stamps, generally with the same design, released by a number of stamp-issuing authorities to mark the same occasion. The British produced, by far, the greatest number of omnibus issues.

In 1953, the governments of the British West Indies and the UK agreed to establish a Federal Government in the West Indies. It came into being in 1958, and comprised ten British West Indian territories. Trinidad and Tobago, Jamaica, and Barbados were the principal members, but the federation included most of the Leeward and Windward islands, then under British control. The seat of government was Port of Spain, Trinidad. Jamaica, the most populous and prosperous member, voted in 1961 to leave the federation, fearing that it would have to shoulder the burdens of the economically underdeveloped members. Trinidad and Tobago followed suit, and the federation was dissolved in May, 1962, the year Trinidad and Tobago gained independence.

Where to Call Home

Here, in Wyoming, where the world
is larger than even unending fields of Kansas,
where one feels more inconsequential
than being lost in dense northern cities.

Here, stray clouds scurrying across
the wide valley are miniatured
between ecstatic mountains
who greet each other like lost lovers.

Here, I am high enough to challenge eagles,
can spread my human arms
and surf the wind's breath,
into the unblinking, weightless sky.

Here, it is safe to take out the stone of my heart,
tenderly caress its multi-layered uneven surface,
slip it into my mouth and feel the fine
crack line where germination has begun.

Here, I shield its fragile enquiry,
hold it close to my breast and listen, again,
to where in these geographical wanderings
it would like me to plant it.

The Vertical of Hope

Slow horizontal tracks,
link distance to distance;
our station,
one decimal in horizon
obliterated by arrival:
Train doors open,
men and women off load
heavy boxes,
suitcases, trunks;
children carrying sleepy dolls
trail behind:
Fathers, mothers, men, women,
march along the platform
with a look of hawk
or determined rabbit.

Like a black and white movie rerun --
future blind -- they hurry past us:
wrinkled, beginning to grey,
me still holding a glimmer
in my gypsy robes,
clutch one-way tickets.
Ready. Our luggage small:
a few old frozen photos:
beautiful wife, handsome husband,
our children young,
ourselves young.

Everything else we own
is condensed into hard, round,
bullets, which we carry

in our throats.
It changes our ease
with words, though we still can speak,
talking of brave-love
which can grow in high altitude
where those who suffer
from vertigo
cannot
go.

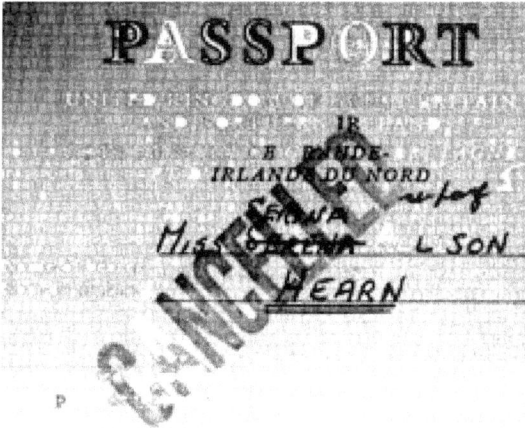

Some Marriages

You said you wanted my fire
yours was missing and you thought
I could fill up the darkness.

I was all fire and was tired
of burning, I needed your coolness
to soothe my flame.

My fire warmed you
and filled up the darkness
but your coolness stifled me
and out went my flame.

Daily Catastrophe

My mother accidentally let the family bird out
by leaving the door to his room open.
Later, she was shocked to find Velvet gone:
The noisy cockatiel who had sung arias
to domesticity, was silent, but she had been
too preoccupied, with cleaning, to notice
either the silence or how bright blue
the sky was that had swallowed him.

My daughter saunters by, eyes narrowed,
her long hair an avalanche of disarray.
"The polluted world!" she reminds me,
"Global warming AND war!" she yells,
"Stupid parents!" she rants.
She never asked to be born, she argues solo;
while I continue to chop onions,
dinner already late and everyone starving.

The garden is overgrown with weeds.
My children's history, and mine,
rescued from the wreckage of divorce,
lie beneath plastic tarps in the yard.
Some bury their dead, others cremate,
I have chosen to compost mine; when one's
sole intent is survival one learns to avert
one's eyes from corpses left to rot in body bags.

Child's Play

I am fishing for a rare word
The etymology of love
Instead your face floats by
Thin like water-lily

The word hides
But your water lily face smiles
And talks dragonfly

I can't hear
Not even my breath
In case the word peeps out
And bites my hook

Rescues me from this child's play
Of trying to name things like:
Flower, baby, cupcake,
Shoe or divorce.

Stepmother Blues

Step-mother watches her step children arrive:
shirts inside out, hair uncombed,
pockets full of sweets which they eat on the sly.
"You can't expect cripples to walk,"
their mother tells their father.

Step-mother makes them groom,
teaches them how to wash clothes,
learn how to cook with olive oil, critiques
cleaning the toilet, talks about initiative,
and how to use a knife and fork at dinner.

Mother says she loves them; at her house
they go to bed when they like, eat what
they like, watch what they like, fight
when they like and if they want her to listen
to disputes they pay her $5.00 a time.

Step-mother insists one will take notes
to his teachers to practice ways to remember homework,
the other she challenges for lying to others
and mostly to himself, the third she keeps silent,
hires a therapist so she will have guidance.

When children leave she sets a candle in her window,
hopes its light will help them return from the woods,
then wraps her arms around their tired
sleeping father's chest and closes her eyes,
prays the forest will be kind.

Sound Barrier

These ordinary days:
love settled into routine,
children, yours and mine,
growing taller
as they place homemade boats
in life's fast river;
breakfast, lunch and dinner;
our fourth fall garden lies
covered in leaves;
inside we are ready for winter
like jets hurtling toward
the speed of sound
over enemy territory.

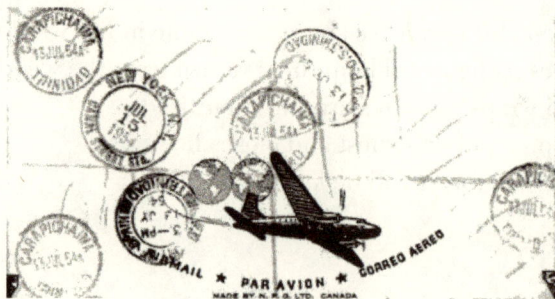

Missing

Suddenly a piece is missing:
only a small piece in the grand scheme,
a pot hole in the otherwise ordinary
landscape of my mouth;
but my tongue frets,
returns over and over to the spot,
like a loved one to the crime scene,
unable to comprehend the irreversible;
whereas before, familiarity
was an unrecognized daily miracle.

Bitter

Some poems don't uplift
they prefer to be nasty
make raw
torture with
sharp glass
until you strike out,
dig a hole,
bury the radioactivity
deep in the ground...
pray that its wicked
half-life does not reach the surface:
seep into the beautiful trees,
the fruit hanging in your love garden,
cause disquiet in the cool shadows
of your tranquil life.

OPENED BY CENSOR

Speculation

I can't quite remember when last I saw her,
no one was paying attention.
Were there danger signals?
Repetitive conversations?
Secrets kept out of a lack of trust?
Or was it a simple case of over confidence
neither realizing the danger
of taking the other
for granted?
What is true is that I miss her.
She had a genuine ability to laugh,
life was a mystery worth pursuing;
she felt special enough to change
the world, do something big.
I miss that she felt interesting, pretty,
a person others would want to get to know,
and keep, I miss how she could be doing the dishes
and suddenly feel inspired to write a song;
I miss how she used to fantasize about true love.
I wonder if I were to call her up
and ask her for a date, for old times sake,
if she'd get all dressed up and meet me
at the local bar? Would we talk
until they kicked us out, like we used to,
myself and me?

Trying to Get Away

I took Madame Bovary to the Adirondacks
where I hoped to view autumnal mountains
paintbrush the canvassed night,
wilderness speak in night loon-treble,
and the pumpkin-faced moon
mimic the rising sun over the lake...

Emma Bovary too dreamed of more
than mundane domesticity;
a villa to view stars...
sunsets bathe in the fragrance of lemons:
in a land where the seeds of happiness —
indigenous to that soil — would bloom,
producing fruits of passion, rapture...

In the cabin I put down self-absorbed Emma
on the bedside table and listen to
my flu stricken husband snore:
Our first vacation in over three years...
Emma and I look for distraction,
we pick up a *New Yorker:*

Immokalee, Florida, it tells us,
forty miles from shell-laden Sanibel Island
is where kidnapped, brutalized,
illegal immigrants are forced to pick

two thousand oranges at $7.00 a day
to make the nation's breakfast orange juice:
Every salad, apple, peach, maraschino cherry,
thanksgiving squash, 4th July watermelon,
our precious Christmas trees
-- sold by corporations --
are harvested by
over a million immigrant workers,
half of them illegal,
all with nobody-status.

Women, too, lured and trapped,
are forced to perform fifteen to twenty-five
sexual acts every day for $3.00 a time.
It's not just the USA, but civilization's face:
Twenty seven million slaves in my bed
on vacation with me
and for once, even Emma
stops thinking about herself.

Saving Us

It was excavation
that brought me here:
rearranging old clothes,
washing others,
making piles that need to move on,
not least the preserving of things,
small,
out-dated,
but too precious, still,
to throw away...
as if by touching
this old pair of pants,
I could remember
the smallness
of my waist then,
under the bigness of your hands,
feet become rivers
as I tried to save us.

Into the West

Through the windshield of inertia –
present and future stretch –
a flat highway through western Kansas:
the road flanked by soybean's infinite
green, capped by unwavering dry skies.
Accelerator pressed to the floor,
you think how you never phoned
your friend whose mother died in spring,
never said you were sorry;
did he need a shoulder,
how was his wife who has cancer?
You want to do it right,
you want to stop the car,
make that phone call, but you don't;
you have that deadline;
besides you are falling asleep,
must use all your focus
to stay awake, not wreck the car.
Now you're too ashamed to call
because if your friend doesn't trust you
who could blame him?
Sadly he's not the only one:
you didn't send those pictures
to friends you visited last summer;
you didn't make time to give your daughter
a promised massage;
tulip bulbs not planted
froze in a below-zero garage;
you didn't remember the woman's name
who smiled and said yours;
you didn't phone the nice couple

you met at a wedding last year
and now the husband's gone and died.
You never called to say good luck
to your neighbour's son who went to Kuwait
to tell him you'd pray,
even though you can't remember when last
you went to church.
You spend all your time working
so you can pay bills,
keep meals on the table –
unavailable even to yourself –
you keep driving
toward the always setting sun,
a stranger in your own life.

Displacement

Having fled too long
loaded with dress sizes too small,
memberships redundant,
points of reference obsolete...
time's river,
eventually,
swollen and greedy
took memory's favorite doll,
names of friends, places;
forgetting made myself easier,
one breath at a time
was all I could
carry.

Transplant

for Bill Hatkie who gardened with reverence

Even the trees in Kansas
remind us that we are foreign
to this love-hate passion between north
and south winds; cold and hot fronts.
Chinese Magnolia will tell
how her delicate velvet pinks,
lured by sunshine and promises,
freeze year after year in Spring,
leaving us to mourn like Lawrence,
after Quantrill's raid in 1863.
Did Kansas promise to be kind to
transplants uprooted by imperialist:
Persian daffodils, Manchurian peonies,
Japanese azaleas, Siberian Iris,
English foxgloves, African daisies and begonias;
Boston liberals, East Coast opportunist,
or slave-owning conservatives,
all of whom weeded out the natives?
Even the concept of garden
conjures images of conquest:
plot of land adjacent to house...
with deed and title to the exclusion
of all unwanted, public gardens
with audience who speak
the language of symmetrical flower beds,
landscaped to make us forget we are in-between Sky
and its beloved Prairie:
Until clouds begin to race and collide,
a brew of green grey swirling tree leaves,
silky stripped petals;
primordial lightening,

hail as large as fists followed by the swollen,
frenzied finger of the sky,
which rips and tears apart the cozy house,
the lovely town, the ornamental garden,
the rake, the shovel, the pruning shears...
the lies, the lies, that Kansas
could ever be owned.

Goddess

The probe carefully entered the dark tunnel,
making sure not to disturb
its fragile landscape.
"Here we are," reports the cheerful technician,
using her ultrasound equipment
to measure geographical features:

There are the nabothians,
and over there like signposts,
fibroids mark the four corners
of this Eden's womb,
over on the North Eastern entrance
the last withered tree
bears a small cyst, the only trace
of a once abundant orchard.

I look at the dark computer screen
illuminated by a Milky Way
of flickering pinpricks of light;
for all I know this is what the
inside of the next undiscovered galaxy looks like.
I wave to the collective on the screen,
I tell them they have been loyal subjects,
though I haven't known a single one personally.

I say I am sorry their planet is dying,
I have no way of stopping the estrogen drought,
calcium deficiency, or atrophy
that is certain to befall them.
They must make the best of what is left,
and be content with knowing

because of them
other universes came into being.
They must know too,
that I am not unaffected,
I, the one they call Goddess
is herself, always the last to know
about the condition of the territories
and am because of them
close to the end
which, I dreamed once,
is only another beginning.

I Admire Their Bravery

The prime minister of Israel
has had a massive stroke, reports the car radio,
another hawk exits the stage of human suffering;
twelve miners found dead in Virginia,
not alive as the jubilant families were told,
although they found goodbye messages written
in the final dark;
another suicide bomb attack in Iraq,
this time 80 dead: arms, legs, torsos
splattered on a canvas of grief.

Our small, self-conscious, pre-teen daughter
gathers up her books for her first day
after school-break
jumps out of the car, without a backwards glance,
to go and greet her peers; wanting so badly to belong
that even after being greeted at a New Years Eve party
with: *What are you doing here?*
You weren't invited!
She walks with determination to meet
the circle of 7th grade girls.

I admire her bravery; the way I admire
those coal miners' wives
who let their husbands go to work every morning;
the way an Iraqi, or Israeli, must rise each day
and wonder if he'll be spared;
the way my friend volunteers one hour
every week at the Humane Society,
walks six dogs, then walks away from the others
in cages, as he walks away from prisoners
he helps in jail but cannot rescue.

I, too, cannot save the world, not even my daughter,
so I put on my indicator, pull out into the lane
of early morning traffic and go on to the next small
part of my day, that only I can do.

Trinidad,B.W.I,

VIA AIR MAIL

to New York

Birthday Invitation

Arriving exhausted, wrung out,
from the navigational push, pull,
through the birth channel;
puzzled strangers greet my nakedness,
speaking languages I can't understand.
I think they are trying to identify
what species I am.

Sun shines through the window,
where I lie cradled, dazzled
by translucent light crystals;
I dream of dancing banyan trees,
wind swept cities in sienna rock,
fields of ocean grasses
laid out on tundra sands.
Parched, I long for glacial springs
descending the Himalayas;
the salty nipples of the sea
as they crest upon
earth's pounding heart.

Half a century later I lie,
still swaddled,
trapped in survival's routine,
have not yet found a clan to claim me;
though the surging tides continue to call,
streams ascend sky, fish fly,
unseen voices whisper,
whisper,
an invitation
every newborn day.

Fragment

As in egg after falling
from time-zone's great wall;
not knowing where you are
or what your name is,
which character are you now
and what are your lines?

As in having the wrong accent,
even in your birth country,
trying to answer your phone
when someone else's rings,
rising in tropical sunshine,
to bed under snow-covered roofs.

As in never having a place to call home,
though you have citizenship of the globe;
people left behind haunt
as if they were dead, not just overseas,
losing step with mortality,
life's metronome.

As you sing each day's nuanced
fragmented song:
      hello... goodbye, hello...
goodbye,   till we meet again...
hello... goodbye....
    I promise to write...
        good-bye... hello...

Mirror Mirror

You said, I should be happy,
after all, I have my health, my children,
a roof over my head...
Yes, I should be happy
like the oyster in her sand bed,
the chimpanzee eating bananas,
the boy flying his kite
and the dog with her bone.

I should be happy.
I should not lie down
exhausted and sad.
The journey's not finished,
I should keep focused on necessities
and the virtue of smiles.
But I was already these things
when we met and wasn't it you who said,
"don't you want more?"
and wasn't it me who said,
"don't be foolish...
                    these are dreams"?

But now it is you who say
"be happy with what you've got";
and "don't be foolish".
And me who cries
for love;
me who the mirror chastises:
grown women should not dream
of knights who want to own forests,
build castles, and rescue
beautiful damsels in distress.

Grown women should be happy
with what they have.
Let young girls dream
about such things,
let them dream,
until they become women
who learn the futility
                        of dreams,
            of castles,
        of knights
and of distress.

33

Four

Angel

**U.P.U. Monument: 1874-1974. Universal Postal Union. U.P.U.
Monument: 1874-1974. Universal Postal Union.** Established in
1874, The Universal Postal Union (UPU), with headquarters in Berne
(Switzerland), is the primary forum for cooperation between postal-
sector players. With 191 member countries, this agency of the United
Nations fulfills an advisory, mediating and liaison role, and renders
technical assistance where needed.

In the mid 1910's A Fredholm, A Stollmeyer and Norman Lamont championed the idea that an agricultural college was needed in Trinidad. Lamont led a long campaign for such a specialist college. In *The Young Colonials: A Social History of Education in Trinidad and Tobago, 1834–1939*, Carl C. Campbell says of the campaign, "Because of his residence and experience in the metropole he was able to encourage the Agricultural society to pitch the campaign for a college at an Imperial level; it was not simply to be a college for Trinidad, not even for the West Indies, but for the British empire."

On January 14, 1924, in the presence of a large and distinguished gathering including members of the governing body of the Royal Botanic Gardens, Kew, London, His Excellency Sir Samuel Wilson laid the foundation stone for the new and permanent building of the recently established Imperial College of Tropical Agriculture in Trinidad. The new building was formally opened in 1926. For the whole of ICTA's existence—up to 1960—the building was the centre of its operations. The building housed the library on the top floor, administration offices including the Principal's, laboratories and classrooms. In 1960, when it merged with the new University of the West Indies, U.C.W.I., the building became the administration centre.

Angel

I found her impaled
in midnight's grey bandages
of mortality.
A garden pitchfork emerges
from her head,
carpenter nails pounded in deep
paralyze her wings, arms;
and a saw blade –
that miracle of technology –
forty-fives below the heart;
keeps her from singing the world anew
as the great Roman road of progress
continues to pave over the memories
of the fallen; their ancient wisdom,
customs, landscapes shattered,
a butterfly, under the hammer
of construction.

Midnight's Room

Aging mother needs property taxes
and house insurance money; her pension
can't keep up with the rising cost of food
and medical bills. In her country,
the over-sixty cannot get health insurance.

Widowed cousin has a rotting roof,
rainy season has begun, the electric bill is late,
unemployment is chronic,
government subsidies turn a blind eye
and she's in constant pain from endometriosis.

Self-employed brother
needs help to pay his credit card debt;
he hopes the bankers will allow him to refinance
his house, reduce inflated interest rates,
and with those savings buy necessities.

Daughter and son's university
fees are due again.
The hundred-year old boiler broke,
insurance will not cover it,
and our bank account is almost in arrears.

Imprisoned by my birthright,
I try to ransom back my family,
work ever faster at spinning straw
in this lonely midnight room of love
hoping to beat Rumpulstilskin
at his blackmail game.

Today I Found Feathers

for Betsy Clark, a bird lover

If I say the words *bird and cat*
a kaleidoscope plays: Happily the bird
often gets away, but if I say *nest of baby robins*
then fear, on soft paws, will stop
your heart when you find a tiny tuft
of feathers attached to bony morsel.

Yes, the nest in the garden pergola is empty.
A neighbor's cat has eaten them.
I mourn for the bereft mother
whose devotion to her offspring
had sustained me while I worked hard
to feed my own children.

I rail at life's harshness.
My only consolation
is that the robin carries on:
She forages for food, is fertile,
can mate and build a home,
reproduce again, love and nurture.

In comparison, what does a fat, neutered,
bored cat have? Except, of course,
the deepest instinct of all: To kill
because it can. Just then a robin flies past
with a twig in her beak,
as she prepares to welcome life.

Restored Victorian

I bought a bucket of *Morning Dew*
and painted windows open.
Toasted Pine Nuts that splattered the floor
were patiently scraped with razor and rags
until the oak grain shone.
Evocative Sunlight in multiple layers
hid bruise marks on the walls.
Two blankets of *Ivory Coast*
covered tenderly mended kicked-in doors.
Frosted-Hawthorn soothed with brush strokes
graffiti from drunken frat-boy parties.
The painted Victorian stood,
as it had for a hundred years and more,
patiently waiting for its wounds to heal.
Next morning I brought a gallon
of *Good As New* and sealed
the front porch done.

Rich

Yes, we are rich with debt
and rich with exhaustion
and rich with the speculation from others
about how rich we are;
rich with sleepless nights in which I toss and turn
wondering how we are going to meet the next
deadline of mortgage payments,
or the next expired 0% credit-card promotion
which will shoot up to 30%
if it's not paid immediately.

We are rich with the breeze
we feel in our faces
as this steam-boat ploughs through
hot and cold atmospheric implosion
on the Grand Rapids of Capitalism;
rich with hope that if we just expend
a little more energy
we'll pick up enough speed to fly over
the thundering economic Niagara
and ski down to the river,
to the open sea and smooth sailing.

Yes, yes we are rich,
sometimes with optimism,
sometimes with pragmatism
but we always know that if
the Cash-Flow gods turn their faces from us
we will capsize
and it will be each man for himself;
and so we keep stoking the fire,
the rich golden fire,

that gives with one hand
and takes with the other.

The Banker and the Artist

for Pat Alexander

He wants to know the bottom line,
how much did you pay
and what have you got in it?
I tell him numbers
off the top of my head.

I ask what's in it for him?
He describes his love,
his art in its raw form, the bottom line:
Money as commodity,
reduction, distillation of energy.

In the beginning there was art,
in the end the artist sold his art.
Why not skip the first stage?
Why not? I ask myself.
Art or money?

Is there a difference,
except in the way we live,
selfishly, or selflessly?

20

Grounds of Incompatibility

Poor Tatania rose one day to find
the drug worn off,
the man she thought she loved
not even a man
but a befuddled ass who had grown tired
of being offered fairy food
when all he wanted was straw.

Consolation Prize

Today, the sky stole my eyes
carried me far into her smile,
lips of golden peach and pink
blew silver dappled clouds,
sunbeams assured my blackened mind
(filled with invisible bat-winged noise):
When all the rainbow frogs,
steelhead trout, and tribes are gone,
its vast lifeless masterpiece
will still stretch across
this exhibition on sure extinction.

50 Years of Airmail in Trinidad & Tobago

In the Family of Mammals

The bat slept,
as it usually did
upside down,
pointy ears pointed down,
small clawed feet attached securely
to a white popcorn ceiling.
Warmth had lured it
into this much bigger,
brighter cave,
but it was day time
and the bat was sleepy.
Therefore, it was not sure
if it dreamed
or if from where it hung,
large, strange, creatures
moved below...
One made a horrible noise
sounding like an animal in pain,
the other scurried about,
stooped shoulders as it rushed out,
a third creature climbed closer,
sudden bursts of lightning flashed
in the bat's sleeping face.

If it was a dream,
the bat was not sure,
the creature with the flashing lights
made a happy gurgling sound;
it made the bat happy
then she heard in her dream,
if it was a dream,

the story of what some do
in tropical climates,
with scotch bonnets
roasted on coal-pots,
to bats' caves;
she didn't like the sound
of pepper smoke.
Then another voice said,
Let the bat sleep
it's her night-time,
we'll move it toward evening
when it naturally wakes up:
After all the bat is family
from the time when we were bats
and nursed our mothers
upside down, or blundered into
someone else's life, announcing,
in all our primal nakedness,
It's me, it's me, it's me,
be gentle.

Five

They Call it Freedom

Hemispheres. Jet-powered Vickers Viking Airliner & Steamer.

Hermes, Globe and Forms of Transport

They Call it Freedom

They were young and proud:
walked without stumbling,
began to invent words,
had acquired a sense of direction,
could tell which fruit were good for eating.

I wanted to fashion them after myself,
strong, beautiful, compassionate,
minds of their own:
yes that was elemental
for self-reliance.

The first lesson, discipline, I thought
they would learn
easiest within our relationship
so if things went wrong
they'd have a safety net.

But they didn't want boundaries in Paradise.
They willed a world outside of me
where danger and suffering
were the necessary alloy
that sharpened their sweetness for life.

I can still hear them laughing and crying
outside the closed gates.
I believe this was the beginning
of what they named freedom:
A kind of tragic ecstasy.

Crossing Over

First the cell divides,
earth opens,
fire pours through
veined darkness into sunlight.

Molecules wind cool,
the spine forms,
nurtured by long nights
mother's milk lullabies.

Rain nourishes DNA kernels;
clouds tell stories of small children
who still speak the language of stars
rivers, mountains and seagulls.

Polar bear and seal cubs eat fish;
tears of wonder moisten fat-cheeked
innocence; blood on scraped knees
mingle with mother's kisses.

The alphabet cross-pollinates
with numbers, language and logic
waltz around life's library,
questions shout to be answered.

Breakfast, lunch and dinner
come at regular intervals
just like the moon, and tidal fluctuations,
the womb ebbs and flows.

While waiting for the barometric pressure

to rise, waters break,
new life incandescent,
mother remembers bridges burn.

Dividing up the Child

She needs punctual meals,
sleep at regular hours,
to dream six-year-old dreams.
Sun should set outside her window
in the same place
but windows, like stations, change every day.

Today her bedroom faces south,
tomorrow east;
she can't remember where she is
when she wakes.
Shoes fall off her feet and hide.

Father's house different from mother's,
and none of them home.
She's dizzy: Will her shoes turn up?
What happened to baby Amanda?
Like a dog who buried a bone, and forgot,
she frets for something unknown...

Father mathematically traveling
in an expanding universe,
Mother searching for her muse,
equitably divided her
between themselves.

Now she erupts with cataclysmic frequency,
"Against what?" they ask bewildered:
Unpredictable sunsets?
The doll she loved and lost?
Her runaway shoes? Growing pains?

My Daughter's Forest

You placed her delicately upon the page,
penciled hands tenderly stroked
the small furry animal she held.
She sat on nothing at all — for you were sure
rocks could not be found in her forest.

I suggested she could sit on a fallen log.
You said that there were no tree stumps
in her forest – men with axes
never went there –   and so she continued
to sit on nothing at all.

Later, because she had grown tired,
rocks appeared to hold her weight.
A blue river ran beneath her feet
and she was content. Then you tried to draw
a perfect mouth. I can still hear your screams.

I told you no mouth is perfect,
they have a will of their own.
The eraser is not an instrument of acceptance;
until you recognise imperfection's possibilities
your girl may never learn to smile.

91

While My Daughters are in Jerusalem
on Sabbatical with their Father

The cockatiel screeches, and screeches;
begs for attention.
I let her out to explore
the Arabian carpet
in my oldest daughter's bedroom.
The solitary fish in the aquarium
gets its morsel of plankton
and I give the cherished guinea pigs
vegetables and water.
I shut their room so the cat can't get in.

Downstairs, the cat scratches
at the kitchen door.
I let him in,
closing it off so he can't go hunting.
Two dogs alerted
come to guard the borders:
It is a cold war of growls
instead of bites and fights.

Outside feels empty
though busy people walk by.
I am here alone, as I was before,
in the traffic jam of survival:
Dog eat cat eat bird eat fish
the world filled only with hunger:
My children, not yet born
to teach about love;
a way to conquer fear.

Confession

for Timmia on her 14th Birthday

I want to give my daughter
a magical amulet;
the kind one finds in the best fairy tale
when the heroine is rewarded
for bravery.

Instead, I yell, frustrated
when she doesn't protect
herself from bullies:
Form alliances like countries, I say,
surprise them with your strength.

The truth is, I have no enchanted
jewel, all alliances deserted me
in my darkest hour; there is
no right way to avoid pain.
Still I watch her, like a blade of grass

grow from bud to flower,
along invisible
chasms between child and woman,
outside the walled fortress
of my love.

Dream Circle

for Zoey, sixteen

Early arrival, a shock of black hair,
the most beautiful new-born
she's ever seen, claims the midwife.
The baby suckles, she sleeps, her sister dances,
her father dances, her mother holds her warm
against her body; soon she'll have to let her go,
soon she'll climb the kitchen stool
like the first prehistoric creature who rose,
stood, and beheld the world with arms held high
like some goddess in a dream, who dreams
she lives the life of a human child,
plays, smiles, cries, loves
and is loved, until one day she stumbles across
doubt's waste land: *Who am I,* she asks,
a goddess dreaming that I am human,
or human dreaming that I am a goddess?

Her sister sings: *Happy Birthday!*
Her father smiles: *Sweet sixteen!*
Her mother wants to hold her warm
against her body and never let her go.
Soon she'll be on that plane, that train, that boat,
she'll walk through those sliding doors
into that waiting room for young travelers;
like the first explorers who sailed into the unknown
hoping to discover new worlds, she'll wave good-bye,
there will be exhilaration in seeking empirical truth.
Inevitably, the discovered
will discover her, they will ask questions:
Are you an invincible goddess disguised as human,
or are you human like us,
living the full seasons of love
which begins with oneself
and leads to joy?

Prom Date

She chose a dress of black,
silk chiffon, cut-out
beaded milky-way overlay
exposed flesh-colored satin,
like gloved mermaid's skin.
A copper crochet bolero
frames night shadows;
crystals illuminate
her gown's starry edge.
In a solitary room
she coiled in and out
long auburn hair,
not unlike Medusa,
whose jeweled serpents
nestled happily
when no one was looking.
On the smooth, tulip softness
of her young face she painted
pools of eye mystery:
fringed misty water irises
and a fan-tail golden hint.

Pink water-lily buds
part into a brilliant smile
as she descends the stairway
to meet a boy
dressed in a tuxedo.

TELEGRAI

Boy in Tuxedo

His awed gaze betrays:
before him stands
all that woman embodies;
if only fear will not stop him
from climbing the tall stalk of virtue
and tenderly removing the glue
that circumscribes
Summer's
fruiting.

On Edge

I want to throw you into the sea
so you can learn to swim,
push you out of the nest before
you have time to be afraid of flying,
but next moment, I'm hanging on in terror.
Perhaps, you won't fly,
you'll just keep on falling;
wind will not lift,
wings will not push down on clouds;
nor will cool water touch
soft and supple,
as you slip and slide like fish;
instead a terrified, stiffened body
will smash hard,
egg on rock.

Instead here I perch
on love's blade,
paralyzed, as I fall
out of guardian mother;
unable to protect you from your demons;
gather you up and coo
soft early morning sunrise,
warm buttered scones, and breathy kisses.
I am only weak tissue stretched
on clumsy bones,
don't know how to let go:
Though all nestlings fly far away,
baby seals embrace frozen oceans,
and even the old, or sickly,
courageously slip on through
the barrier in between.

Tomorrow's Hope

Bedrooms are museums, now,
filled with childhood artifacts:
Each doll, animal, bird, fairy prince,
or even blue iridescent painted drift wood
waits in suspended animation;
stories, air bubbles, encapsulated
in the glass blower's art.

The doll's house children
have been skiing for six years;
parents, aunts, uncles
wait at home with babies and toddlers,
my grown daughter tells me,
because she and her sister could never decide
what their children looked like.

The small stuffed pig rescued
by the parish priest on a rickety ladder,
after she parachuted off the turret
of a tenth century Roman church in Essex,
my daughter sobbing on the ground below,
now lives among the other old-age pensioners
telling, and re-telling past adventures.

Soon their voices will be muffled from inside
cardboard boxes where childhood is buried
along with lost jewels, cities, dragons, babies...
in the darkness that is dust to dust,
in the darkness of forgetting,
in the darkness of books not opened,
in the darkness of tomorrow.

Holding Your Breath

When the caterpillar goes into the pupa stage
it will spin a hard layer around
its soft baby flesh, seeking darkness
in a secret world, where irrepressible drummers
call time to a different tune.

Every molecule will rearrange itself
into a new configuration inside
that mummified shell it shows the outsider.
Gone are days of green-veined sunshine
when feet, like hands, clung to the newness of living.

We all know what happens next.
One day when no one is looking
the shell will split to reveal the changeling:
Her wings still crumpled, skin dazed
by cool air against her trembling body...

You'll hold your breath wondering can she fly?
Will she be lucky and escape predators,
find the best nourishment; fall in love
with the right one, let you go in peace
before your drummers come to call time.

Threshold

Timmia, eighteen

Dawn waits, everyday she waits,
everyday a new leaf uncurls somewhere,
a child is born, a relative dies,
the tadpole finds its legs,
and the toddler discovers the sky from a swing.

Mother waits, she waits with her belly big and round,
everyday is one day closer to the appointed time:
she works while she waits,
she is making stars for her child,
yes, stars, horses, and birds of prey.

In the beginning there was silence;
we all stood by the port-hole of darkness
and while we waited we hummed stories
of distant wars, lovers' journeys,
triumphs, disasters, and of beauty:

Icarus falling, feathers snowing the sky,
ancient temples return sand to desert,
a grandmother tells of revolution
to her orphaned grandchild,
fields of flowering weeds blanket unmarked graves,
clay shards of extinct tribes lie glistening among
the lacy remains of once giant conches;

Mother waits, they all wait,
for the child to arrive, to open her eyes
and see what gifts have been given:
Pegasus flies over clouds, peacocks flash

aquamarine, flowers bud and bloom, frogs chorus
the carousel of creation.
Dawn waits, she waits each morning,
while mother waits her daughter grows up;
her boat has crossed the threshold, as she goes
she hums stories of hope to the orphans,
teaches how brave one has to be to see
both beauty and the beast inside ourselves,
then she dances with dolphins.

Signs of Life

In this big, old, perfect house,
restored so that you can't see the scars of a hundred years
only designer paint that hides uneven plaster
casting memories, room to room,
of buttered scones, translucent water, autumn's dusk.
I meander through silent hallways
waiting to hear the wooden staircase creak...
I hold my breath, listen long, ears twitching in the air
like a hunter on a deer's trail;
a door slams in the distance and I turn just in time to see
the fleeing shadow of a young woman disappearing into night.

In the morning roses hung to dry
lie scattered on the cold granite kitchen counter top,
red petals startle the chilled air, I look at the empty twine noose
then back to the stone slab, a loaf of bread has been opened,
butter shows the indentation of where a knife has passed,
a few crumbs trail toward the shut door,
my eyes follow the light along the back porch,
then steps into the garden, invisible under a shower of leaves.
I turn back and stare at the bread crumbs.
Hansel and Gretel never stood a chance,
neither does the witch.

After work I return to the big, perfect Victorian house
restored so that I can hide behind its hundred years of walls,
meander through the mirage of make believe home
waiting for the house to give up its secrets;
maybe it will be the sound of hushed giggling,
the sudden buzz of a transmitter searching for its frequency,
a window banging in the attic,
unfamiliar puddles on the kitchen floor,
the swish of soft feet trailed by fabric,
or the sudden rare phenomena of my daughter's face
eclipsing the doorway with a smile.

Ouroboros

To live alone one must be an animal or a God – says Aristotle.
There is yet a third case: one must be both – a philosopher.
                                                Nietzsche

No one else from your childhood
saw you go down to harbour
where your ship waited to sail.
You said you didn't like good-byes
so, yes, coming to see you was for me.

This gift of diaphanous white curtains
and scalloped-quilt for your cabin;
mirror-waves hung on walls
in which you will see only yourself, not me,
these small touches were as if I was giving
one last home-made birthday cake,
one last piece of doll's house furniture,
one last tuck-into-bed.

I was saying bon voyage to my beloved child:
who goes to what discovery?
what adventure? heart ache and joy?
what multitudinous fortunes?
It was about me being there
to see the rising of your star,
as I was when you first appeared;
then to leave the empty skin
of motherhood behind
and swallow my tail.

Notes on Poems

Poems are woven from words; words are not only multilayered in the etymological sense but nuanced through cultural lenses. I have chosen a random assortment of words from certain poems to elaborate on, whether to give a definition or simply to include background information as a way to deepen the reader's understanding.

Long Distance:

Murano: a tiny island that has been home to the glassmaker's industry of Venice, Italy, since 1291.

Orinoco: one of the longest rivers in South America (1,330 miles). Its delta empties into the Gulf of Paria, a shallow inland sea between the island of Trinidad and the east coast of Venezuela.

Lokono: also known as Arawak, is the name of the indigenous people who live along the eastern coast of South America, once including Trinidad. There are roughly 16,000 Lokono still living today, mostly in Guyana.

No Sound was Heard

Sapodilla: an evergreen tree of a genus of about 80 species in the family Sapotaceae. It's distinctive taste has been compared to a combination of pears and brown sugar.

The Twenty Fifth Hour

Bromeliad: Any of the flowering plants of the Bromeliaceae family, with almost 2,600 species. All but one species are native to the tropical New World and the West Indies. Many bromeliads are short-stemmed epiphytes and are often known as air plants because they have no attachment to the ground or other obvious nutrient source.

Straits of Magellan

Agouti: rodent species related to guinea pigs which looks similar but bigger and with longer legs.

Scarlet Ibis: Trinidad & Tobago's national bird:

"At sundown, some 10,000 of the vermillion-feathered, migratory waterfowl return from days spent in Venezuela, just nine miles away, to roost in the mangrove swamp south of Port of Spain...

"The scarlet ibis can often be found in less majestic circumstances ... conservationists say that eating scarlet ibis is merely emblematic of a country cannibalizing its natural resources through voracious industrial growth."

> POSTCARD FROM PORT OF SPAIN, (Trinidad)
> On the Menu: A National Treasure by David Shaftel
> TIME in Partnership with CNN.WORLD

The Sun Never Sets

At the peak of its power, it was often said that "the sun never sets on the British empire" because its span across the globe ensured that the sun was always shining on at least one of its numerous territories.

Tate and Lyle were two separate cane sugar refining operations in Britain. In 1921 the two merged to become Tate&Lyle. Henry Tate had already been knighted in 1897 for his considerable philanthropic deeds, which included the founding of the National Gallery of British Art; also know as the Tate Gallery. In the mid 1930's Tate&Lyle began to purchase land and set up production facilities in Trinidad, Jamaica, Belize and Mauritius. In 1975, Tate&Lyle ceased its operations in Trinidad and the Trinidadian sugar industry was nationalised and sugar production was incorporated under the name Caroni Ltd.

In July 2003, the government closed Caroni Ltd and ended the production of sugar cane after centuries of farming. 77,000 acres of arable farmland still sits idle. 20,000 people working in sugar production were made jobless; this figure does not include Caroni contractors, ancillary staff and private sugar cane suppliers.
GDP - composition by sector: agriculture: 0.5%

Manifesto

The **Pitch Lake** of Trinidad is the largest asphalt reservoir in the world, discovered by Sir Walter Raleigh in 1595 from which he used tar to caulk his ships. It is 250 feet deep at the center and contains between six and ten million tons of the tar like pitch. In 1800 the lake became the largest supplier of asphalt to the world. An estimated nine million tons have been removed.

Oil: Trinidad produces 163,000 barrels of petroleum a day; just under 1% of the United States' daily oil consumption.

The population of Trinidad & Tobago is approx. 1,240,000. It has one of the smallest growth rates in the world and the second highest GDP in the Caribbean. Oil and gas account for about 40% of GDP and 80% of exports, but only 5% of employment.

Post Immigrant Recipe

Gingerbread House: In Trinidad, a Painted Lady in Distress. Published: November 12, 2008, by David Shaftel, *New York Times*.

106

"...Even the Magnificent Seven, a row of famous colonial buildings including a French Baroque mansion and a castle inspired by the one at Balmoral, in Scotland, represent a random assortment of styles, in various states of repair. But perhaps no building on the Savannah is more emblematic of Trinidad's chaotic history than the Boissiere House, a 1904 cottage as majestic as any of the mansions and a rare example of turn-of-the-century Trinidadian architecture.

"Like something the Brothers Grimm might have conceived, the house has a large gabled dormer separating two Chinese pagoda-like pavilions, marble steps, and intricate fretwork. As John Newel Lewis, an English architect, wrote in "Ajoupa," his 1983 book on Trinidadian architecture, "The whole effect is magical and nostalgic with mysterious colors and a melancholy air. The house is an example of Trinidad's visual heritage at its best.""

"Nicholas Laughlin editor of the Caribbean Review of Books, said "The Boissiere House is part of the imaginative reality of anyone who has lived in Port of Spain, and I had become horrified by buildings that I thought would always be there, that are an indelible part of the city, disappearing".... "

Birthright

Obeah: a ritual or system, found mostly in the French and British West Indies, of secretly held beliefs in the use of supernatural forces to attain or defend against evil; it is African in origin and varies greatly in kind, requirements and practice.

In her 2007 article "Crossing Troubled Seas: The Metaphor of Flight in Caribeean Literature," which she presented at King's College, Dominique Aurelia quotes Helene Christol as writing: "Such echoes of the cultures and rituals from Africa point to the attempt to tame the "strangeness", the deregulation of the universe, thus incurring a subtle interplay between continuities and discontinuities, ruptures and fusions, the ontological objective being the restoration of order preceded by its disruption."

One such echo was the belief that after death the spirits of the slaves would fly back home, to Africa. Aurelia goes on to say that, "Those who had kept the gift of flight, those who remember, must transgress their suffering bodies and through the process of metamorphosis dismember their bodies. During slavery (or enslavement, to quote Earl Lovelace) the slave's body belonged to the master who used it as a tool, an object. But he did not own the slave's soul. To be free is to have power over one's own body to be able to manipulate it, to transform it and create new flesh and bones... The one who flies has chosen freedom instead of amnesia. To fly is to remember."

In her novel *Wide Sagasso Sea*, Caribbean author Jean Rhys' protagonist, Antoinette, is white, however, home to her is her birth island in the West Indies. Hers is the island of strong, independent, black Christophine: nanny, adopted mother, and spiritual support system; and Tia, daughter of a house servant, whom she has a complex friend/enemy relationship with.

Antoinette's whiteness does not does not prevent her from absorbing myths and cultural ways from her surroundings. These myths are from Africa, and from the Amerindian/pre-

Columbian natives. They are ways of coping with the diaspora she, too, is born into. When Rhys describes Antoinette's final moments, or rememberance, about Coulibri, her home on the island, before she leaps to her death, she describes how her hair "streamed out like wings" (pp.189-90) wings that would take her home to freedom.

Where to Call Home

According to the 2000 U.S. Census Bureau, 164,778 Trinidadians and Tobagonians reside in the United States, of which 75,583 live in New York. 24,000 live in the United Kingdom (National Statistics, U.K.); 50,000 live in Canada (Canadian Census); 1,260 live in Australia, and an additional 640 claim to be of T&T ancestry, either alone or with another ancestry (Australian Census).

At least 240,038 Trinidadians and Tobagonians live overseas, and, except for the Australian census, which identifies offspring with T&T ancestry, this figure does not include offspring born on foreign soil.

Dr Bhoendradatt Tewarie, Pro Vice Chancellor of the University of West Indies, was quoted as saying in Trinidad and Tobago Newsday, Jan, 2007: "Trinidad and Tobago is facing one of the worst brain drains that this part of the world has ever experienced." He said that among the education of Guyana there is a 77 percent migration rate; in Jamaica and TT it is about 50 percent and "on a per capita basis the brain drain from the Caribbean is the highest in the world..." He went on to quote from an article in the Financial Times (March 23, 2005), stating that "Trinidad and Tobago was identified as having the third highest brain drain in the world."

The lowest population growth rate, – 1%, is now reported from the south European state of Montenegro. HIV/AIDS has placed two African nations, Zimbabwe and Swaziland among the countries with the lowest population growths – 0. 78% and – 0.41% respectively while emigration had resulted in a – 0.89% growth rate in the southern Caribbean republic of Trinidad and Tobago. (United Nations Nations Unies) Population of the twin islands is approximately 1,240,000 million.

Transplant

Quantrill's raid: The town of Lawrence was established in Kansas Territory in 1854 by antislavery settlers. It soon became the center of proslavery violence. By 1863, Kansas had long been the center of strife and warfare over the admission of slave versus free states and became known as Bleeding Kansas. Quantrill's pro-slavery group of about 450 men descended on Lawrence in a fury at dawn on August 21st,1863, two years after the Civil war had started. Over four hours, they pillaged and set fire to the town and murdered most of its male population. Quantrill's men burned to the ground one in four buildings in Lawrence, including all but two businesses. They looted most of the banks and stores, as well. Finally, they killed between 185 and 200 men and boys out of a population of approximately 2000 people.

Angel

Extinction threshold: a term used by conservation biologists to explain the moment at which a species or population, experiences a qualitative change in density because an important parameter, such as habitat loss, or migration, is reached. It is at this critical population size below which extinction probability increases.

According to *BBC* science correspondent Corinne Podger, reporting in 2002, a quarter of all mammals face extinction within the next twenty or so years. Migration os species to habitats not native to them, along with the continuous spread of human settlement, the destruction of wilderness, rainforest, and wetland regions, and industrial impacts are some of the major causes of this predicted loss of biodiversity. A United Nations Environment Programme report identified over 11,000 endangered animal and plant species. This includes nearly one in eight bird species.

Ouroborous

The Serpent biting its own tail was first seen as early as 1600 BC in Egypt. From there it moved to the Phoenicians and then to the Greeks, who called it the Ouroborous, which means "devouring its tail." Similar symbols appeared all over Europe, Asia, Africa, China, Australia and Japan, as well as in North and South America. The Aztecs, American Indians and South American peoples all had a variation.

In *Les Structures anthropologiques de l'imaginaire*, (Paris: Bordas, 1969), Gilbert Durand says it is "the greatest symbol of totalization of opposites".

Plato, in *Timaeus*, described a self-eating, circular being as the first living thing in the universe — an immortal, perfectly constructed animal:

"The construction of the world used up the whole of each of these four elements. For the creator constructed it of all the fire and water and air and earth available, leaving over no part or property of any of them, his purpose being, firstly, that it should be as complete a living being as possible, a whole of complete parts, and further, that it should be single and there should be nothing left over out of which another such whole could come into being, and finally that it should be ageless and free from disease. For he knew that heat and cold and other things that have powerful effects attack a composite body from without, so causing untimely dissolution, and make it decay by bringing disease and old age upon it. On this account and for this reason he made the world a single complete whole, consisting of parts that are wholes, and subject neither to age nor to disease. The shape he gave it was suitable to its nature. A suitable shape for a living being that was to contain within itself all living beings would be a figure that contains all possible figures within itself. Therefore he turned it into a rounded spherical shape, with the extremes equidistant in all directions from the centre, a figure that has the greatest degree of completeness and uniformity, as he judged uniformity to be incalculably superior to its opposite. And he gave it a perfectly smooth external finish all round, for many reasons. For it had no need of eyes, as there remained nothing visible outside it, nor of hearing, as there remained nothing audible; there was no surrounding air which it needed to breathe in, nor was it in need of any organ by which to take food into itself and discharge it later after digestion. *Nothing was taken from it or added to it, for there was nothing that could be; for it was designed to supply its own nourishment from its own decay and to comprise and cause all processes*, as its creator thought that it was better for it to be self-sufficient than dependent on anything else. He did not think there was any purpose in providing it with hands as it had no need to grasp anything or defend itself, nor with feet or any other means of support. For of the seven physical motions he

109

allotted to it the one which most properly belongs to intelligence and reason, and made it move with a uniform circular motion on the same spot; any deviation into movement of the other six kinds he entirely precluded. And because for its revolution it needed no feet, he created it without feet or legs." [emphasis added]

NOTES ON ILLUSTRATIONS

CONTENTS

I   **BRITANNIA**: sits on bales of sugar with ship waiting in background, issued during Queen Victoria's reign: May 1819 – 22 January 1901.
PAQUEBOT: on the agenda of the 1897 meeting of the Universal Postal Union held in Washington D.C., was what to call and what to do with mail posted on the high seas. Most international agreements of the 19th century used the French language, as it was the recognized language of diplomacy, so the use of the word "Paquebot" meaning "packet boat mail" was adopted. Other Paquebot markings used were "Posted on Board", "Ship Letter", "Ship Mail", "Packet", "Posted at Sea", and "Posted on the High Seas."

II   **POSTED ON BOARD**: marking on ship-carried mail. 1837 Royal Mail Line opens first steamship service between England and the West Indies.

III **TRINIDAD TO LAGOS**: Hand stamped first cover, air mailed, 7:45 a.m. Dec. 7th, 1941. Pearl Harbor is bombed 7:53 a.m. Pacific time.

IV   Stamp showing the **Memorial Park** monument in Port of Spain which commemorates local soldiers who served during WWI and WWII. WAR TAX: Cancellation stamp. Antigua, Dominica, Grenada, St Kitts- Nevis, St. Lucia, British Honduras and the British Virgin Islands all issued war stamps in 1916; Barbados, the Cayman Islands, Montserrat, St Vincent, Trinidad & Tobago and Turks & Caicos followed suit in 1917.

V   The university was founded in 1948 as the **University College of the West Indies** (UCWI) at Mona in Jamaica, in special relationship with the University of London based on the recommendations of the Asquith Commission, established in 1943, to review higher education in the then British colonies. Subsequently, campuses were established at St. Augustine, Trinidad (1960) and Cave Hill, Barbados (1962).

ONE

Looking at Her

3   **LMcL stamp, April 1847, was the first adhesive stamp** to be printed outside Britain, and the first in the Colonies: The Trinidad stamp featured the *S. S. Lady McLeod,* a paddle steamer that carried mail between San Fernando and Port of Spain, from September, 5th, 1845, until 1854.

5   **SHIP-LETTER TOO-LATE**: postmaster stamp to show letter had been delayed.

7 **CANCELLATION MARK**, late 1800's: **Obliteration** 1) Another word for cancellation. A cancel that is particularly, and intentionally destructive to prevent any chance of re-use of the stamp.

11 **22** was the postal cancellation mark for Claxton Bay, 1881. There were 35 districts bearing the official postal marks of the post office of origin.

12 **SHIP-LETTER TRINIDAD**: Earliest record of a ship-letter is dated 1848. "...It will be remembered that Trinidad was surrendered to Britain by Spain on February 18th, 1797, and this was confirmed by the Treaty of Amiens, 1802. During that period a boat had been used to carry the mail between there and Grenada at a cost of £500 per year.... A further note (C.1808) shows that by then six Mail Boats were being used for the local service, at a cost of £7,776 per annum. "The amount of letters delivered by these boats outwards is between £9 and £10,000 per annum: the returns may be estimated at the same." L. E. Britnor.

13 **U.S.NAVAL STATION**: Chaguaramas was home to the United States Navy during WWII. Their discarded 55 gallon steel oil drums was part of the birth of Steel pan.

17 **PAN AMERICA WORLD AIRWAYS** was founded by the world's first airline tycoon, Juan Trippe. PAN AM was the first to fly the Pacific, first across the Atlantic, and first around the world. It first visited Trinidad in 1929. In **1931 Piarco** Airport openend. This 1946 letter is hand stamped to commemorate "Direct Clipper Flight New York to Trinidad".

TWO

Atlas of my Birth

21 **BOAC British Overseas Airways Corporation** (BOAC) was the British state airline from 1939. On November 16, 1954, it visited Piarco, Trinidad, during a proving flight. Financial trouble forced it to close in 1962 and the government of Trinidad purchased aircraft from BOAC for the **BWIA** airfleet.

22 Stamp in British Passport made by the **British Consulate in Trinidad**.

24 6 cent stamp depicting **Sir Walter Raleigh and his discovery of Lake Asphalt** which he used to caulk his boats. Cancellation mark appears later to commemorate 1967, five years after **Independence, 1962**.

27 **Postal First Day Cover commemorating sugar cane farmers 1882-1982,** cancellation mark *Buy Trinidad Sugar.*

30 **Aerogrammes**: The official Universal Postal Union designation for an airletter sheet. Aerogrammes are written on and then folded to form their own envelope. They are delivered for less than the airmail rate. No enclosures are permitted. The United States has ceased to use them.

36 **BY AIR MAIL**: Sticker obtained from post office to show that postage is sufficient to cover air passage and not be sent by ship. The USPS no longer carries such stickers as letters are no longer carried by ship.

45 **Six stamps depicting local scenes** in new **W.I. dollar currency issued in 1935**:
First Boca, Imperial College of Tropical Agriculture, Memorial Park, Town Hall,
San Fernando, Queen's Park Savannah, Government House, Port-of-Spain

BUY TRINIDAD SUGAR: Sugar industry closed down in July, 2003, by PNM
under Prime Minister Patrick Manning.

THREE

Where to Call Home

50 **QUEEN'S PARK HOTEL**: built in 1895, torn down by British Petroleum Amoco
Oil Company in 1997 to build its ten story headquarters. The only reference I could
find posthumously about the demolishing of the Queen's Park Hotel was an article
by David Wondrich, in **Esquire**, about the famous Queen's Park Swizzle, a rum
cocktail: "None of these were more handsomely verandahed (is that a word?) than
the Queen's Park Hotel, where everybody who was everybody who came to
Trinidad stayed. You can't stay there now, though -- they tore it down a couple of
years ago to build their headquarters. Port of Spain's just that kind of town. At least
the Swizzle lives on."

54 **VIA AIRMAIL * PAR AVION * CORREO AEREO**: These English, French, and
Spanish words adorned the bottom of airmail envelopes to differentiate from letters
sent by ships. They have now become obsolete as all letters go by air
internationally.

56 **OPENED BY CENSOR**: During World War II, Trinidad's position on the South
American airmail route as well as its geographic location meant it became a
regional center for censoring mail to/from South America. Postal censorship
primarily takes place during war-time or periods of unrest.

62 **Registered letter**, **Aug 13, 1868**: Any prepaid letter, news-paper, book or other
packet for any place in; New Zealand, United Kingdom, British Colonies, and many
other foreign countries, may be **registered** at any Post office, during office hours,
on payment in stamps affixed to the letters.

67 **CORONATION OF QUEEN ELIZABETH** II: 1953 Omnibus series issued to all
British Colonies; each country would insert its name onto identical keytypes.

73 **33** was the postal cancellation mark for Maraval.

FOUR

Angel

80 **Surcharge Postage**: Trinidad was the first British colony to initiate postage due
adhesive stamps. It was used to collect fines on unpaid or insufcently paid mail.

83 **50 Years of Airmail in Trinidad & Tobago**: Fall, 1929, Charles Lindbergh accepts

112

Juan Trippe's offer to become chief consulting engineer for Pan American Airways and help expand its air routes deeper into the Caribbean. Approval by Congress of the increase in air mail appropriations asked by the U.S. Post Office Department are an important factor in the financial progress of the Pan American Airways, Inc., the main operating unit of the Aviation Corp. of the Americas.

FIVE

They Call it Freedom

89　On 26th September, 1929, the first airmail was flown out of Trinidad and Tobago. On behalf of Pan American Airways, Charles **Lindbergh** flew from Miami to San Juan in a Ford tri-motor aircraft, and then in a Sikorsky S38 to Dutch Guinea - routes FAM 6 & 10. He made 17 stops before he returned. This became known as the Lindbergh Circle.

93　**TELEGRAM**: The world's first telegram was sent on May 24, 1844 by inventor Samuel Morse. In 1871 the first telegraph cable was laid (at Macqueripe Bay) linking Trinidad with the rest of the world. **On January 27, 2006** the last telegram was sent by Western Union; forms of electronic communication such as email, fax, instant messaging and text messaging have made the telegram obsolete. The message posted on Western Union's Web site without fanfare was "Effective January 27, 2006, Western Union will discontinue all Telegram and Commercial Messaging services. We regret any inconvenience this may cause you and we thank you for your loyal patronage."

"The 'universal' Royal Mail service, which delivers letters anywhere in the country for one price, has made a loss for the first time in 160 years. Chief executive Adam Crozier said that without urgent help, the service will struggle to survive.

The company's latest results, published yesterday, show the service, which he called "a vital bedrock" and "part of the fabric of our society", lost around £100 million last year."
　　　　　　　　　　　　　　　　MAILONLINE by Becky Barrow, May 2008

"The U.S. Postal Service lost $297 million in its first fiscal quarter, ended Dec. 31, ...
"This situation, coupled with the growth in electronic alternatives to mail, creates a very challenging environment." "
　　　　　　　　　　　　Thomas L. Gallagher I Feb 10, 2010 7:52PM GMT
　　　　　　　　　　　　The Journal of Commerce Online - News Story

Serina Allison Hearn

Photograph by Mario Freue,
another admirer of our endangered Leatherback turtles,
taken at Grande Riviere, Trinidad,
May 2009.

Serina Allison Hearn

Born, 1957, in Trinidad, where she attended Bishop
Anstey Junior and High School. Hearn studied fashion at
St. Martin's School of Art, London, UK, and opened
her design studio under the label Serina Hearn Designs.
1980 -1988 her haute couture designer ball gowns
were carried in venues like Harrods, Knightsbridge,
London, U.K.

Emigrated to New York, U.S.A. in the late 80's.
Here she began to use the building blocks of words,
her first love, and poetry in particular, to debrief and
recompose her evolving identity due to former
continental leaps from Trinidad to the UK and
then to more nomadic explorations in the USA.

She now works in the restoration of historic Victorian
houses in Lawrence, Kansas, and continues to invest
in their sustainability by leasing them as homes.

Her first book of poems, Dreaming the Bronze Girl,
published by Mid America Press in 2002,
was noted as one of the top 100 books, 2002,
by the Kansas City Star.

About the Artists

Timmia Hearn Feldman is a Theater Studies major at Yale University. She directs, writes, acts, and aspires to dance. Since she was a child playing with finger paints, she has found little as fulfilling as the act of creating two-dimensional art. In between plotting her next show, and staring absently out the window, she works for the Yale South Asian Studies council and teaches English to children at a child refuge in Nepal.

Justin Shiney is a silk screening acrobat who can print on anything, including wood and glass. He operates an independent studio - Shiney Independent - and offers his customers integrity and human warmth; something hard to find in the mechanized commercial world of printing. When he isn't trying to keep up with his customers demands he's a family man who loves fishing.